Fascinating Food Chains

Grassland Food Chains

By Marybeth L. Mataya
Illustrated by Hazel Adams

Content Consultant
Jacques Finlay, PhD, Assistant Professor
Department of Ecology, Evolution, and Behavior,
University of Minnesota

magic wagon

visit us at www.abdopublishing.com

Published by Magic Wagon, a division of the ABDO Publishing Group, 8000 West 78th Street, Edina, Minnesota 55439. Copyright © 2011 by Abdo Consulting Group, Inc. International copyrights reserved in all countries.

Looking Glass Library™ is a trademark and logo of Magic Wagon.

Printed in the United States of America, North Mankato, Minnesota.
042010
092010
 THIS BOOK CONTAINS AT LEAST 10% RECYCLED MATERIALS.

Text by Marybeth L. Mataya
Illustrations by Hazel Adams
Edited by Nadia Higgins
Interior layout and design by Nicole Brecke
Cover design by Kazuko Collins

Library of Congress Cataloging-in-Publication Data
Mataya, Marybeth.
  Grassland food chains / by Marybeth L. Mataya ; illustrated by Hazel Adams.
     p. cm. — (Fascinating food chains)
  Includes index.
  ISBN 978-1-60270-795-5
  1. Grassland ecology—Juvenile literature. 2. Food chains (Ecology)—Juvenile literature. I. Adams, Hazel, 1983- II. Title.
   QH541.5.P7M38 2011
   577.4'16—dc22
                              2009051195

Table of Contents

A Grassland Food Chain

A food chain tells who eats what. It shows how living things need each other. Let's find out what's for dinner in the grassland!

In one grassland food chain, big bluestem grass comes first. A prairie dog chomps on this plant. But the little animal is also food. Soon, a black-footed ferret eats it up. Then, high above, a golden eagle soars. It swoops down and attacks the ferret.

Grass to prairie dog to ferret to eagle. That's a simple food chain. But a shaggy bison also grazes on big bluestem grass. Another food chain begins. Together, food chains connect into food webs.

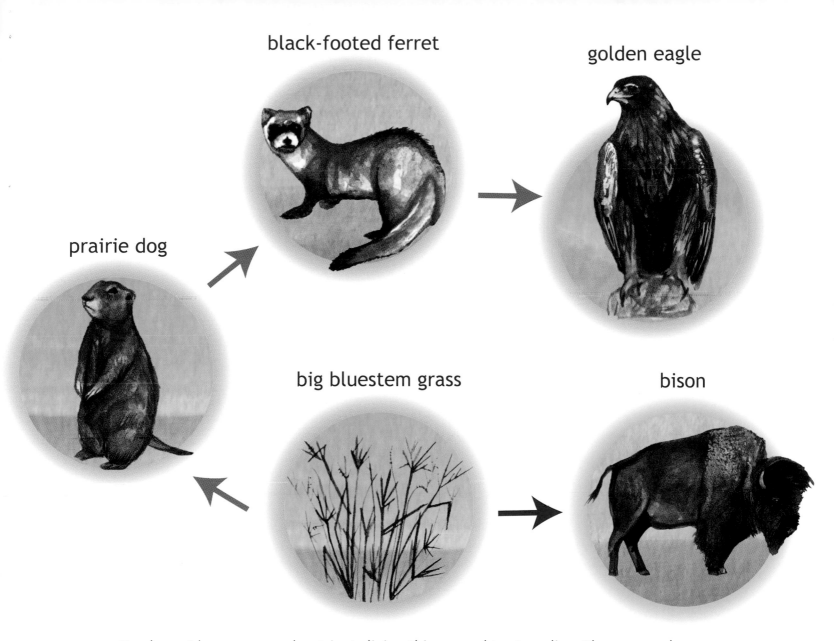

black-footed ferret

golden eagle

prairie dog

big bluestem grass

bison

Food provides energy and nutrients living things need to stay alive. The arrows show which way nutrients and energy from food move through a grassland food chain.

A Sea of Grass

In a grassland, wild grasses grow as far as the eye can see. Few trees grow. The tall grasses sway in gentle waves.

In North America, grasslands are called prairies. These grasslands are hot in the summer and cold in the winter. In the spring, melted snow and heavy rains water the land. Many kinds of plants and animals live here.

Prairies once stretched across the middle of North America. They covered land from Texas through Canada.

Plants Come First

Sunflowers and other plants are at the bottom of a grassland food chain. That means they don't eat other living things. Their roots drink up rain and melted snow. Their leaves soak up the bright prairie sun.

Prairie plants take in as much sun as they can. Sunflowers turn their flower faces to the sun. Compass plants turn their leaves toward the blazing sky.

Herbivores Eat Plants

A prairie dog hops out of its tunnel. It munches on some blue gamma grass. Not far away, huge bison graze. These animals are herbivores. They eat plants. They are the next link in the food chain.

Prairie dogs live in "towns." They build mounds. They dig tunnels and rooms under the ground.

Carnivores Eat Other Animals

A black-footed ferret waits by a prairie dog's tunnel. When the little animal pops out, the ferret attacks. Nutrients and energy from the plants the prairie dog ate now fuel the ferret's body.

Animals that eat other animals are called carnivores. They are the next food chain link.

Black-billed magpies are birds that are carnivores. They eat the ticks off bison.

Top Carnivores Rule

The ferret is full from its prairie dog dinner. It is too slow. A golden eagle dives down and grabs it.

The eagle is a top carnivore. It hunts other meat-eaters, such as the ferret. Top carnivores are fierce. Few animals dare attack them.

Top carnivores also eat the young of other carnivores. Baby ferrets, weasels, bobcats, coyotes, and golden eagles have to watch out.

Omnivores Have Lots of Choices

Prairie chickens snatch up seeds and grasses. They also swallow wandering insects. Some animals eat both plants and other animals. They are omnivores. They find lots to eat in the prairie.

People are also grassland omnivores. They hunt prairie chickens and harvest sunflower seeds. They can cook bison steaks on the grill.

Fire!

On a hot summer day, lightning strikes the ground. Suddenly flames burst among the grasses. Some animals are caught in the fire.

But fire helps the prairie's grasses. It keeps other plants from taking over. The grasses grow better than before. Herbivores grow fatter. So do the carnivores that eat them.

The Cold, Cold Winter

In fall, the air grows chilly. Prairie birds such as meadowlarks fly south. Snakes, badgers, and some prairie dogs burrow underground. They will sleep through the winter.

The other animals work harder to find food. Mice tunnel through snow to gather seeds. Bison use their hooves to paw up grasses. Owls fly farther to hunt.

Decomposers Clean Up

In the spring, a golden eagle dies. It lies on the ground. A fox comes to eat the bird's dead body.

Afterward, worms, beetles, and bacteria swarm on the leftovers. They also feast on animal waste and rotting plants. These tiny creatures are called decomposers. They clean up the grassland. They break down the last bits of food into nutrients for the soil. In turn, the rich soil helps plants grow.

Brown-headed cowbirds follow bison. The birds eat the decomposers that gather on the bison's waste. Another food chain starts.

23

People and the Food Chain

For thousands of years, American Indians of the prairie hunted bison for food and fur. They also collected prairie plants for food and medicines. American Indians have great respect for the plants and animals of the prairie.

Indian healers made teas from purple coneflowers, black-eyed Susans, and other plants. The teas were used as medicine.

Today, very little of North America's prairies remain. The grasslands had rich soil. So farmers dug them up to plant crops such as corn and wheat. Cougars, grizzly bears, and wolves were hunted until they were mostly gone. Cities sprang up where prairie dog towns used to be.

Prairie dogs are very important to the grassland food chains. Many animals eat them. Others live or hide in their burrows. But prairie dogs are in danger in many areas. If they die off, other animals that depend on them may also be lost.

To protect prairie dogs, learn more about the prairies and their food chains. Then you can tell others how important and interesting they are!

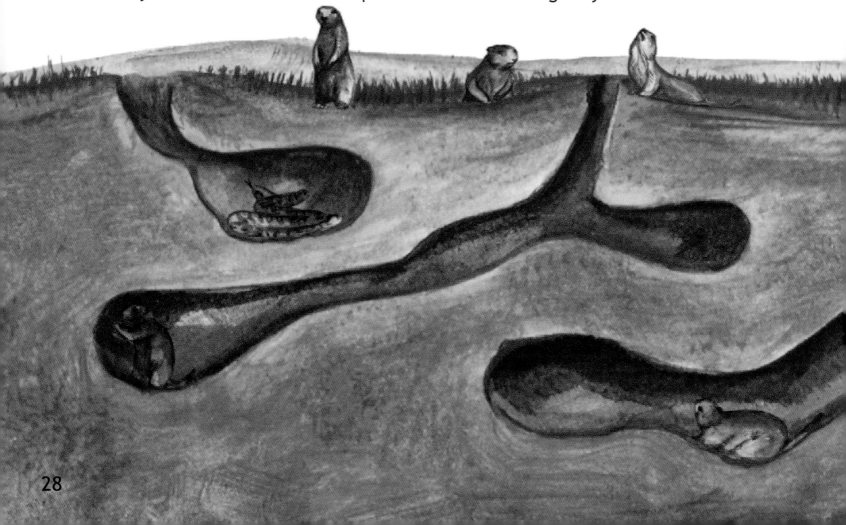

At home, you can grow prairie plants such as blazing stars, sunflowers, and black-eyed Susans. They attract prairie butterflies.

29

Food Chain Science

Scientists study grassland food chains and food webs. They want to learn about all the ways plants and animals are connected.

Plants that aren't from the prairies, such as crabgrass and ragweed, can take over the prairies. They disturb food chains. So scientists burn grasslands that have been taken over. Then the prairie plants grow back. Scientists replant prairies, too.

Cattle can also hurt the prairies. They graze too much in one spot if they aren't moved often. Scientists are working with ranchers for ways to keep cattle moving. Another option is to raise bison. They don't cause the same problem as cattle.

Some American Indian groups have tried to care for prairie plants and animals on their lands. They have worked with scientists to bring back animals such as bison, swift fox, black-footed ferrets, and prairie dogs. Scientists have also done this in public parks and lands.

Fun Facts

An adult prairie dog eats about 25 pounds (11 kg) of grass per year. It takes more than 400 prairie dogs to eat the amount of grass one cow eats in a day.

Scientists think that 40 species of mammals, 90 species of birds, 80 species of plants, 29 species of insects, 15 species of reptiles, and 10 species of amphibians are connected to prairie dog towns.

A single black-footed ferret will eat about 100 prairie dogs a year.

In a tall grass prairie, grasses can grow as high as 7 feet (2 m).

Grasslands with a scattering of trees are called savannas.

Grasslands have many different names, such as veldt in Africa, steppes in Russia, and pampas in South America. Every culture and country has its own name for grasslands.

More than 200 plant species can occur in a wild prairie of just one square mile (2.6 square km).

Words to Know

bacteria - tiny living things that help break down dead plants and animals. Bacteria can only be seen with a microscope.

carnivore - an animal that eats another animal.

decomposers - tiny living things that live on the dead remains of plants and animals as well as animal waste.

energy - power needed to work or live.

herbivore - an animal that eats plants.

nutrients - chemicals that plants and animals need to live.

omnivore - an animal that eats plants and animals.

top carnivore - a carnivore that is not preyed on by other carnivores.

On the Web

To learn more about grassland food chains, visit ABDO Group online at **www.abdopublishing.com**. Web sites about grassland food chains are featured on our Book Links page. These links are routinely monitored and updated to provide the most current information available.

Index